HANNAH LOWE

CHAN

KU-782-705

BLOODAXE BOOKS

Copyright © Hannah Lowe 2016

ISBN: 978 1 78037 283 9

First published 2016 by
Bloodaxe Books Ltd
Eastburn
South Park
Hexham
Northumberland NE46 1BS

www.bloodaxebooks.com
For further information about Bloodaxe titles
please visit our website or write to
the above address for a catalogue.

Supported using public funding by
ARTS COUNCIL
ENGLAND

LEGAL NOTICE

All rights reserved. No part of this book may be
reproduced, stored in a retrieval system, or
transmitted in any form, or by any means, electronic,
mechanical, photocopying, recording or otherwise,
without prior written permission from Bloodaxe Books Ltd.

Requests to publish work from this book
must be sent to Bloodaxe Books Ltd.

Hannah Lowe has asserted her right under
Section 77 of the Copyright, Designs and Patents Act 1988
to be identified as the author of this work.

Printed in Great Britain by Bell & Bain Limited, Glasgow, Scotland, on
acid-free paper sourced from mills with FSC chain of custody certification.

CHAN

Core Collection

Do Not Withdraw

NEWHAM LIBRARIES

9080010 1081126

Hannah Lowe was born in Ilford to an English mother and Jamaican-Chinese father. Based in London, she has worked as a teacher of literature and creative writing, recently completed her work on a PhD, and is now a lecturer in Creative Writing at Kingston University. Her first book-length collection, *Chick* (Bloodaxe Books, 2013), won the 2015 Michael Murphy Memorial Prize, and was also shortlisted for the Forward Prize for Best First Collection, the Fenton Aldeburgh First Collection Prize and the Seamus Heaney Centre Prize for Poetry. This was followed by two pamphlets, *R x* (sine wave peak, 2013) and *Ormonde* (Hercules Editions, 2014), and her family memoir *Long Time No See* (Periscope, 2015), which she read from on BBC Radio 4 Extra in 2015. *Chan* (Bloodaxe Books, 2016) is her second book-length collection.

for Richard and Rory

ACKNOWLEDGEMENTS

Some of these poems or earlier versions of them have appeared in the following publications: *Compass Magazine, In, Jamaica Journal, Magma, Morning Star, London Magazine, Poetry, Poetry London, The Rialto, Rising* and *The Yellow Nib*.

The poem sequence *Ormonde* has been published in a chapbook, *Ormonde*, with accompanying visual and archive material (Hercules Editions, 2014).

My sincere thanks and gratitude to Mimi Khalvati and members of her workshop; and to Bill Herbert, Betony Lowe, Kenneth 'Honey' Lowe, Vici MacDonald, Richard Price, James Procter, Alan Robertson and Tammy Yoseloff.

I am also very grateful to Newcastle University, the University of the West Indies and The Chinese Benevolent Association of Jamaica for their time and support.

CONTENTS

BORDERLINER

What I Play Is Out the Window!

If You Believe: Ribs

If you believe I saw Joe Harriott play in 1956
and in my good blue dress, danced all night
in that basement dive below Gerrard Street,
Joe howling through his sax, white shirt
sweat soaked and gleaming in the spotlight,
you may as well believe any of the things
I dream on, listening to his music –
the way he smelt up close say (of cigarettes
and clove) when we took a corner table
at the *New Friends* on Salmon Lane, gnawing the ribs
he loved and in between chews just talking
to me in that fatherly way he had.
You may as well believe that sometimes
I put his records on and just start crying
and can't stop crying, don't even know
what I'm crying for – those decades in history
when men like Joe and my father were shadows
on English streets, or just the way
a melody can get you. I walk the small rooms
of my flat, light spilling through the skylights,
the treetops just in sight through the glass
and even with all these tears, I'm sort of happy.
Richard says be careful what you do in poems
to real people (*known* people), but surely this poem
shows its seams enough to let me wish
that Joe didn't start dying so young (at gigs
he couldn't even stand up straight to play),
that men he used to jam with didn't see
his broken body shuffling down the streets
and turn away, and those last morphine days,
the dog he saw barking at the window
of the third floor ward really wasn't there –
well, how could it be, if Joe and me just stepped
from the club into this winter night,
heading arm in arm down Brewer Street
to order steaming bowls of wonton soup?

Sax I

That gold horn hung out of you nightly
like a distended tongue – the fix you craved
at The Sunset Club or on The Blue Room's stage
or the 'generous' hours you played
in backroom jams, oh boy, you needed it.

Rajah, Theorist, Sire, the way you saw yourself,
that gold bone stuck out, perked up by hot white girls
on stools who lapped you up, but the sex that night
was solo, Joe, eyes closed, your throat wide open,
walking alone, the gold road to heaven.

Sax II

Joe, go down for Beaujolais, or send 'your woman' down.
The landlord knows that liquor's yours.
Now close the door. Now breathe, now drink.
Now lick the reed. Now flick it.

That white girl's riding buses back across the town.
Put down your cup. Lift up your baby from its velvet snug.
Bellyful of blood, now blow that gold, Joe blow it!
What you play is out the window, out the room.

Cherokee

I was playing with fire

BET LOWE

He phoned me up, a party, would I go?
My mum said *Joe who's Joe, a darkie, no!*
Not on your nelly, lady, no you won't you −

Peach lipstick, lacquered beehive, Tweed Mist perfume.
I took the bus and 'course there was no party,
just a room with whiskey glasses on the bedside

and fag ash on the tangled sheets at dawn.
Oh Joe could play an ace − *The Akee Blues*
and *Cherokee*, dah da-da deeee dee!

He put his sax in hock to pay the rent,
said *Betty can you help me*, had a pound
off me on Sunday nights, he had it bad,

he'd not been with another girl in weeks
he said, and no, my mother didn't sleep
a wink, she sobbed into her mixing bowl!

Then off to Auntie Connie's caravan,
he wore his suit and wingtips on the dunes,
he said he loved me in the spinning teacups

then vanished in the night. He knew a tune
that bastard arsehole drunk − *You'll Never Know*
and *Cherokee*, dah da-da deeee dee!

And no, I couldn't bring him home for Christmas,
Not over my dead body, lady, no!
He came with flick-knife smile and lilac bath cubes

and oh she sobbed into her mixing bowl!
My father walked him to the tube, came home
and stank of whiskey, said, *he's just like any*
other fella, ain't he, Betty, ain't he?

14

Pinewood Suite, unrecorded, 1958

Joe Harriott, in bed above the pines!
You cannot blow a note now, splutter petals
all bloody in the sax's throat and bell.

No puff to poeticise or soar, no girls
to magnetise. Just pretty nurses padding
with rubber soles and clipboards, Savlon smiles,

their chin-wipe-keep-you-supine eyes, you're bed-bound
with a view of pines, deep green, so green you dream it,
and that old sedition itching in your head –

you've only what the kinder matron brings you:
a red ink biro, ruler, cartridge paper,
your hand-drawn stave, ('Our Mr Harriott

is indisposed but *is* composing'). Hacking
through the weeks until you slip the ward, then home,
no puff for anything but cigarettes,

a woman in your rooms with tissues, pillows
tomato juice, and television re-runs –
Chan Canasta palming cards or reading minds,

your sax laid flat upon its back below
the bed where you are trussed in dressing gown,
a twitching hand that might not be your own

discharging notes that race like fire ants
across the page, up and down and round,
so wild and fast not even you can catch them –

Quintet at a Party, 1960

Upstairs, we were discussing rhythm and atonality.
Women floated
      in beige chiffon
            down the bright hall.
There were trays of tiny slips of toast
      with single prawns, a snip of cress.

Joe said: *It's like painting sound.*
      Think of the abstract expressionists.

He kicked the door shut. This was private.
      Think of Hans Hofmann, he said, hands spread.
Coleridge shook his head
      and I said *hmmm*,

my thoughts sliding through the door
      and down the banisters
            to where that black-haired
                  green-eyed woman stood,
                      her head thrown back.
      Her teeth were white, her throat was white,
she wore a tight rope of chubby pearls.

      I couldn't see through walls
but knew next door
      Shake was at the bookcase,
swigging from his flask

      and downstairs Phil was hidden in the pantry
with a giggling girl who held his sticks
      and drummed the shelves.

He held an upturned spoon,
      was crushing uppers for their soda –
baby pink, lavender, sky-blue.

Song for Shake

When I was born
my father gave to me
an angelhorn
with wings of melody

SHAKE KEANE, 'Angel Horn'

At six, he strutted with a polished trumpet
on the steps downtown, sunlight on his glasses.
Shake for the Shakespeare he loved
or the 'Chocolate Milkshake' song.
At twelve, he led his brothers in a swing-band –
four rawbone boys hop-steppin' on the parched lawn
of the tenement, the bailiffs looking on.
Leaving, he stepped lightly – a notebook
for his poetry, his father's dented horn,
a history play. When I was born

they nearly called me Harriet for Joe –
another island man in England. On stage,
his saxophone manoeuvred round Shake's flugelhorn –
the way two neighbours one day gossip sweetly
at a garden fence, then next day argue fierce
about who owns the breadfruit tree.
They licked those notes with something
of the islands – the syncopated breeze of soca,
mento, or the old calypso rhapsodies
I knew as gifts my father gave to me.

Shake played in every hazy dive in Soho –
the Feldman, the Flamingo, on ads for *Spam*,
a little bossa nova with the Hastings Girls' Choir;
came back from Europe *all played out*, his hip-flask
never empty. Went home to *gutsify* the island,
fix the *bodderation* – his swollen-belly laugh, a foghorn
blowing into Kingstown. What came to pass?
A notebook scrawled with angry satire
and crotchets spat like peppercorns
across the page. Still he played an angelhorn

17

and took it with him to New York, no visa,
just the easy warmth of Tiffany's Lounge
with its solitary drinkers, and Shake most afternoons
snug in the corner with his poem-book, a newspaper.
Whichever fellow slammed his face
into a fire door one evening on Pulaski,
maybe didn't mean to wreck his embouchure.
Old snow-beard giant, there's sunshine through
the glass today, and on my stereo you play for me
your angelhorn, with wings of melody

Partita, 1968

When the tabla and double bass are really moving,
        the raga in full swing,
I think of when I used to run for hours, for miles

        out of the door in my old bent trainers,
early winter nights, the streetlamps flickering on –
        heel-toe, heel-toe –

through Clapham, Balham, and down the hill
        to Tooting Bec,
men in white robes on the white temple steps

        a child eating with her fingers
in a canteen strung in Diwali lights,
        smell of cumin on the cold black air.

Sometimes I think Partita is the girl
        on the album cover, and all the musicians
are in love with her.

        Only Joe is really free, stood
at the Five-Note bar alone –
        black suit, white shirt and saxophone.

When the trumpet plays, half-muted,
        something like a fanfare, something like a party horn
(we called them twizzlers or fandoozles, flid whistlers)

        I remember turning back on the Common,
the houses lost from sight,
        stumbling on tree-roots, listening

to help me see –
        heel-toe, heel-toe –
past a man on a bench, smoking in the dark,

        a freight train stalled on the bridge,
a dog, all shadow,
        springing out across my path.

What Is and Isn't Jazz?
(found)

Mr Harriott & his cohorts
are shaking everybody up

with what he calls his 'free form' pieces,
        his 'abstract compositions'

        but

I find myself at the end
of the shortest patience in these islands
with Mr Harriott.

Can something with form
        really be free?

If it is 'abstract'
        who could have
                composed it?

To my ear, it is the woolly din
of a batch of sick sheep
squelching through a quagmire in hail

        interspersed

        with stretches

        of drab boredom.

Mr Harriott's laboratory tests
are in the early stages

        and though
        he should be admired
                        (perhaps),

does jazz need constant broadening?
        Are fresh kicks desired daily?

Mr Harriott, stop crying
        through your horn
                and start playing again,
                please!

If You Believe: Old Paradise Street

If you believe I played with Phil Seamen in 1970,
a Sunday night, The Dog and Bone half empty,
Phil just keeping time with his sticks in one hand
and then, when the punters flocked in,
his hands a blur on the ghost notes and flams,
you may as well believe anything I dream of
looking at his old album covers –
how on the bus to gigs he'd beat a Yoruba groove
on his knees, or mine, while the passengers stared,
one knee the high-hat, one the snare
or how we drank the night down in the flat
on Old Paradise Street, his record player
spinning through Ghana, through Cuba,
Phil just tapping his feet or later, a fag spilt
from his half-moon heroine grin:
Don't you know at midnight I turn into a pumpkin?
Rack-thin in his old cardigan, drooped
in his chair, but what he knew about drumming
was like opening the door to let the sunshine in.
Or you might as well believe that last try
at getting clean, stood on the Burton canal
with his fishing pole or strolling the streets
where the boy he'd been had thrown
the windows wide and whacked his drums
over the backyards and washing lines,
had nearly set him right – 'Phil's Renaissance'
Melody Maker said of the gigs we played
if you could sugar-coat the sweats and sores, the sick.
Who'd guess a nap in his chair would be
the good long sleep? Worn heart, barbiturate-weak.
Goodnight Phil. There's a bright moon tonight
on Waterloo, and the hiss of vinyl on your turntable
spinning spinning the long night through –

Ethology

If alto sax players could ever have been genetically developed
from some sort of amoeba millions of years ago, then Joe was that.
He wasn't really a person.

SHAKE KEANE

Like green amoeba are always
green amoeba, or the cat
can't help herself chase sparrows

                              (in Skye, the pier at dusk,
                              that shivering mongrel, jumping
                              through the freezing water
                              every time we threw an empty can),

so Joe kept playing – the shabby pubs
in seaside towns and working men's clubs
where he slumped and had to sit to play

                              and like the animal who disappears
                              to die alone, he packed his sax,
                              clean bandages, a tie, went limping
                              through the midnight terminal.

Mingus

Charles Mingus on the ward at midnight, come
through rain and hail in dripping gabardine
to matron, standing firm and handing him
a pen. *A note? Say what ma'm? Please. Goddam.*

Alpha Boy

Blind Lemon, Mojo, Fire-In-His-Soul-Joe,
back down the corridors to boy-in-shorts,
your hand in Sister Susan's hand, your mother
gone, your brother gone. Behind the gates
you learnt the Alpha Sisters' prayers and hymns,
their discipline – dawn bowls of hominy
for Bad Boys, Hellions, the Pitiful,
but listen!
       Down the moonlit hall the sound
of clarinets and flugelhorns and through
a keyhole will I find you Joe? Horn raised
to below-blow, or cuddled low to make
the brass cry, sweet-sad din that made you good
at *something*. Lying in the cloistered cells
the Sisters knew their Alpha Boy could swing.

All the Bodies in the Foreign Ground, 5000 Miles from Home
(for Richard)

My forgotten second cousin lies at Bitterne –
antique stone church five miles beyond Southampton,
and Friday found us knelt and foraging
in roses (sweet of you to help me), looking
for his grave. He wasn't hidden on the fringes
in the end, not secreted in vines or grasses,
oh no, we saw him by the sunlit path,
a marble headstone with an epigraph:

Parker?
>   *There's them over here*
>>   *can play an ace or two.*

                    I'm thinking of the woman who had read
                    about Joe's funeral, who came and stood
                    alone beside his grave, blue passion flowers
                    in her hands. She didn't even know him, never
                    listened to his music, no, she'd only come
                    to be among the crowd, a face from home.

Coda

Travelling jazz man?
  That one good suit's
    no good no more.

If You Believe: One Pale Eye

If you believe I met Chan Canasta in 1962
after hours in the cold at the stage door,
Canasta sweeping through in his long black coat
as I called out *Sir? Sir?* and he turned
and loomed above me like a vampire,
you may as well believe any of the things
I dream about, watching his old TV shows –
the way he handled a deck of cards up close
(they couldn't catch it with the camera)
like pulling a silk scarf through his fingers,
or the Slavic ghost in his voice, conducting
his guests to pick a card, or think of a card
but *please ladies and gentlemen, keep it secret*
or how he held them all in the corner
of one pale eye, and you knew somehow
he had read their minds. You may as well believe
that night we walked down by the canal
was the first of many times – the narrow boats
in their carnival colours moored in the mist,
the smell of tar, and Chan not looking at me
but talking, talking, as though I was the first person
to ever ask him – of the family in Cracow
lost in the war, of the shaded roof garden
in Jerusalem where he had read book
after book on occultism and mesmerism
and practised his experiments –
if you have talent you must polish it until it glitters
and how he remade himself in Britain –
pilot, magician, English-Polish gentleman.
Was it the first light coming up
brought silence? We sat by the lock,
Chan pulling his cards from his pocket
and holding each one up to his lighter
until the flame spread and the symbols
and faces cindered, and he flung them out
across the dark still water, like firebirds.

Ormonde

Ormonde

Rewind, rewind the *Windrush*! Raise the anchor
and sail her back, three weeks across the water
then let the travellers disembark, return them
to their silent beds at dawn, before the mayhem
of the docks at Kingston Town and Port of Spain –
they'll wake to see their islands' sun again.

Wind back the hours, the days and months, a year –
and out of fog, *Ormonde* sails, like a rumour
or a tale of how a disremembered thing
will rise again – light up, awaken engines
and swing her bow through half a century,
return a hundred drifters, lost at sea.

Among the crowd, here's Gilbert Lowe, a tailor,
strolling starboard with his wife and daughter
or staring out to sea alone most nights
here's Paul the Carpenter, the yellow moonlight
and his battered playing cards for company
or curled like woodlice in the canopy

of darkness under deck, those stowaways
who'll leap for Liverpool on landing day
and sprint a half a mile of stormy water
in suits and shoes, to climb the slimy timber
below the Albert Dock where policemen wait
to haul them off before the magistrate

and all the passengers step from the ship
and through a coverlet of mist, then slip
like whispers into tenements and backstreets
as *Ormonde*'s deep horn bellows her retreat
and from this little piece of history
she slowly creaks her way back out to sea.

What I Know

This shaking keeps me steady. I should know.
What falls away is always. And is near.
I wake to sleep, and take my waking slow.
I learn by going where I have to go.

        THEODORE ROETHKE, 'The Waking'

At night, you find me at the oil-lamp, dice in hand.
I say to myself, if I throw a pair of fives
I'll give up this life – the hot slow days
of hurricanes, sweet reek of banana rot,
black fruit on the vine. I want another hand
of chances. I grip the dice and blow
a gust of luck into my fist. I'm dreaming
of England, yes, work, yes, women, riches.
I shake these bone cubes hard, let go.
This shaking keeps me steady. I should know.

The radio fizzes news across the tenement yard –
dazed soldiers sailing home, a weekend parade,
monsoon time coming. I pass dead horses
in the field, dead mules. Men sag like slack suits
in the square. Talk of leaving starts like rain,
slow and spare, a rattle in a can. My tears
aren't for the ship, new places, strange people,
but the loss of my *always* faces – I mean,
my people, who I know, my places. My sister says
you carry them with you, don't fear.
What falls away is always. And is near.

The ship rocks steady across the ocean.
You ever look out to sea, and on every side
is sky and water, too much too blue?
Thoughts lap at me like waves against the bow,
not where am I, but why and who?
At night, we use our hours up, ten fellows
flocked to someone's sticky room. I roll the dice
or deal for chemmy, brag, pontoon.
We go till dawn, a huddle at the lamp turned low.
I wake to sleep, and take my waking slow.

Some fellow swore there were diamonds
on these streets. Look hard enough in rain
you'll see them. I squint my eyes but what I see
is sunshine on the dock, my mother's white gloves
waving me goodbye. There's no diamonds here,
or if there are, they're under this skin of snow.
Seems the whole world's gone white. I roll my dice
in basements below these English pavements.
I guess I'm learning what I need to know.
I learn by going where I have to go.

Passieras

We were losing memories already.
They slipped like fish into the blood-red water.
My daddy's limp, that crazy bougainvillea,
the savage rooster crowing on the fence.

A hot sea wind lulled us past Havana.
In the dark church below deck,
Hosco sang and strummed his banjo.
We danced calypso, samba, limbo,

swigged rum until a fire burnt
in every one, and we christened ourselves,
Passieras, Passieras, drifting
on the world's high curve.

We were frontiersmen, we said.
Our god was work. What use was memory?
Ships in the night blinked back our lights –
we glided on, eyes fixed to sea.

Boxer

brother, one week in
your footwork's
slippin'

let's do roadwork on deck
skip there too
keep jumpin'!

keep out the lounge
at sundown
those fellows don't

got the chances *we* got –
time for high-jinks
on the other side

Mr Alexander
paid our fare remember?
you best keep punchin'!

I've chalked a ring
the moon's our floodlight
I'll be running laps

come get me
when you ready
we'll go toe to toe

if you won't
spar with me
I'll fight my shadow

Dressmaker

At night, I made myself a dress for England.
All through the rainy months, I stitched by hand,
a silver thimble on my thumb. No more
my threadbare skirt or patched-up pinafore.
By candlelight, my pattern was a map
laid out across the bed, and as the rain's slow tap
became a lightning storm, my scissors traced
the pattern line – long sleeves, a gathered waist,
one tier of voile, one poplin, double-skinned
for England's winter time, and the cold sea wind.
It changed my shadowed figure on the wall.
I dreamt myself – on a red bus passing Whitehall
or walking on the Strand. There was a tea-room
where I wiled away my idle afternoons
and in every scene I wore my dress, bright red
for pillar box and rose, the robins pictured
in my books at school. And now, at the ship's cold rail,
I am a dash of colour in the grey as we sail
still closer and closer, and finally I see
through a veil of cloud – England, my destiny.

Schoolboy

didn't see her
when i said goodbye
no light she said *get going child*

gon buy a cricket bat
in england
shoes and school

but i don't care
she sold my pig
for the ticket

coughing in the yard
to rope him
nightie hanging off

franky walked me
to the harbour
shook my hand

now it's sea sea sea
they gimme jokes and mints
and call me 27 bitten street

because she sewed it
in my shirts in navy cotton
before – when she could sew

someone i never met
will look after me
in england

her voice whispering
from the corner
say please   sit still   be good

Gloves

My mother wore a thimble made of copper.
My mother was a seamstress or a chamber-maid,
or market-girl or nurse or cotton picker,
or a washerwoman, fingers blistered red
from strangling sheets in lime and washtub water.
She disappeared through linen on the line
and like a mocking bird, I heard her laughter –
a teaspoon on good china, lady-fine.

My mother was a photograph. Her name
was *Longing* or *Desire*. She stumbled south
along the Parish Road, barefoot and shamed
in dirty lace, gin bottle to her mouth.
My mother was a hand in a long white glove,
the moment before the glove was pulled off –

Distressed British Seamen

MOFFATT: I knew black men at Tiger Bay – sea dogs
from Cape Verde, Somali skippers. Now this lot
quiz me: *England this or England that?* Some nights
they light the deck with songs – my foot tap taps.
But other nights, I tell them let me rest.
I am a seaman and distressed.

PAGE: Of all the portside misses she was darkest.
She laid a trail of birdseed and I followed,
clambering up into the sweetest nest.
Oh seven days, bedridden frangipani!
Please sail me home, I've not a penny left.
I am a seaman and distressed.

HOOPER: You shoulda seen the other chap! This shiner
ain't a patch on what I done to him. I'll go
a round with any boxer from Tobago
or Jamaica. I'm a British bulldog! I'm a –
I knocked the policeman out, I slugged the jailor!
I'm a seaman and distressed.

WILES: What the wife will say? This pustule bubbles hotter
every day, and now my palm and soles
a'scratching like there's hungry ants inside,
a weepy rash across my back and chest.
I'll see an English doctor 'fore I'm dead!
I am a seaman and distressed.

SAEED: I stewed a vat of *pulpo* on my stove,
the brine so lightly spiced with cumin, clove.
Saeed, they said, you are the best of chefs
before each sailor retched into the sea.
That's it for me, my spoon is laid to rest.
I am a seaman, and distressed.

Stowaway

A dirty neck. One shirt, each day more grey
might easily give men like us away
because we took our passage unencumbered –
no clothes, no coin. Eleven was our number,

eleven tucked into the *Ormonde*'s hold,
and how compliantly the body buckled
if a crewman's footstep fell – we'd quickly twist
into a cask, we sad contortionists.

We couldn't bear the hopeless day-long yawn
of home, and had no gold or pearls to pawn,
no cow or goat to sell – but as we'd hands,
we'd work, and if a ship set sail for England,

so we would stow away. And we were fed
by kindness – serviettes of scrap, old bread,
some fleshy bones. One passenger bestowed
a laundered shirt on me for mine had yellowed

and when at last the docks on England's rim
rose up, what choice had we but to jump and swim?

Johnny Cakes – A Recipe

For tree-shadow lunch and labrish,
sunk-belly sleep, till you rise and pick

or for easy penny pickney-filler,
stuff your baby's cheeks, and quick

or if your son's a tall boy sailin' off
for England (your heart gone doughy-thick)

fry him johnny cakes with stewed tomato,
gungo peas, scotch bonnet kick

or wrap him johnny cakes in muslin
for the ship – a taste of home, last finger-lick

or if you are a just-come man
in Liverpool, alone alone and heartsick

in a dirty room, the windows steamed,
rain trickling down the naked brick

and all you do is dream of flying back?
Well, grease your pan to stop it stick

and rub together flour, water, sugar, salt
a johnny cake may do the trick –

In

In Liverpool, you walk the dock for hours
In your bag, a box of dominoes, a pair of brogues
In the street, a little girl tut-tuts at you
In your belly, worry rising like the wind, but hold it boy, just hold it
In the tenement house, a bed you swap with other men
in shifts, you pass the afternoons
in dreams: the rooster on the fence, your sister's twisting hands, the smell of   uh
In *England*, you're in England
In the shop, a rock of last week's bread you carry home
in snow, your slipping soles and god knows how the world went white like this
In the street, a woman frowning, crossing over
In your pockets, nothing but a letter, flimsy blue
In the labour queue, ten men ahead the same as you – you're in, you're
in, no, no, some other fellow's in, new worry rising like a wind
In the glass, a thinner picture of your face
In your dreams, a yukka moth, a shell, the sea
In the back room of a pub, a cheer, the pint glass clunk   just hold it boy, just
In the makeshift ring, a shirtless man who looks like you, but *something*
in your pocket, *something* in your pocket
In the air, your bare fists flail, his bare fists crack on your cheeks, your lip   split
in two, a glug of blood, your blood, oh
in that gloomy room, a single bulb above the ring, the arms you're sinking like a puppet
in

Ship-breaking

These folks were not the victims of migration…
these folks mean to survive

STUART HALL

I watch old films of shipyards on the Clyde:
cranes ripping ships apart, their metal hides
peeled back by men in goggles wielding fire.
The shock of innards: girders, joists and wires,
a rusted funnel toppling in slow motion.
Those open flanks rain down the cabin's foreign
detritus of flags and posters, turquoise charts
of distant oceans, photographs of sweethearts –

They tore the *Ormonde* up in '52
for scrap. I google what I can. If you
were here, you'd ask me why I care so much.
I'd say it's what we do these days, Dad – clutch
at history. I find old prints – three orphans
on a deckchair squinting at the sun; a crewman
with an arm around a girl, both smiling, windswept;
a stark compartment where you might have slept

and I recall that old trunk in our attic –
cracked leather, rusted clasps – *my box of tricks*
you said, you said you'd lost the only key.
Your home, the ship you sailed, those miles of sea
were locked inside. And now my mind replays
a ciné-film: the young man on a gangway –
the trilby tilted, pocket hankie, his smartest gear
and his stride so well-rehearsed – it says *I'm here.*

Mishra's Blues

I

We are all sad men, with our one-pan meals –
my turmeric-sardines, your scotch-bonnet sardines!
Even the saffron stains on my counter
are a gasp for home. Chan, do you ever –

        think to go back?
    Sure, Mishra. Some days the city give me big adventure,
        some days cold shoulder – so lonely
  I cry at my own friendly face in the mirror.
        But Mishra, come, when you feel blue
  what's worse than talk of home
        or to read your granny's weep-weep letter?

She says my grandfather is sick with a fever! She says –

        Stir me some chai now, Mishra.
    How 'bout the radio? Let's play a little hand
        of Baccarat, warm our bones in here
    while out there it snows and snows, and –

damn this British weather
keeping customer at home!

(they play)

II

        You know Mishra, me never think to ask
  but you have a cousin or some-such in Jamaica?
        Name Misir? Like Mishra, give or take?
  While I sit here watching you losing, the long face
        getting longer, I remember Misir –

Misir? Who are you talking of Chan?

Misir! Is fifteen years since I saw him
        on the path home from school
when that cruel boy Luther take the slingshot
        Misir won from teacher –
boy Mishra, was Misir a good speller!
        But Luther trap him under the mango
and hurl stones into the branches to rain
        a storm of fruit on Misir head!
Him dancing, so skinny and fast
        as the mango bust like stars on the dirt
till one hit him hard and down Misir went
        and Luther thieved him!

Oh I can still see him face
        so blue, with him slingshot gone
and your sad face just now remind me –
        poor Misir look *just like you*!

Me? Are you flimflamming me Chan?
Play your card! See those tigers on my wall,
the elephants in green mirror?
Their eyes are fixed to your hands,
you sharpie, you swizzler!

        Cool it Mishra! Just asking is all!

(they play)

III

Though, thinking a little more on it Chan,
some Mishras went a long time ago from Lakimpur
to Trinidad, Tobago. Seven-year cane cutters.
No cousin of mine, but great-great aunty and uncle,
married on the coolie ship! Mama had a photo –
two white-robe oldies, holding hands
under a cane field tree, strangers to me,
their sad eyes staring somewhere far.

Chan, I fear things will come to pass
the same way here, seven years
becoming twenty years becoming –

        one hundred years! Mishra, I know how it goes
            and Trinidad not close, you know
      but near enough to wonder how Misir turn up
            with your face in Yallahs Bay, Jamaica.
      Like the big ship sail in all directions
            dragging poor folk from one place to another

And I too, Chan, am a good speller,
not like those plantation clerks
with their negligent pens!

        how we end up here man?

      me thinking your chai spice taste
            like the sweet tea my own granny made me
      when I was a boy with a bung nose and cough

      and in England my body feel well
            but still I drink this draught, and can't get enough

      and now I read in a book the old tribe Maroon
            up in the Blue Mountain had a spirit language

      and say *chai* did mean 'carry'

(they play)

46

Borderliner

My Father's Notebook

(found)

I do not know the exact date of birth,
       of arrival to the island.

He hardly ever spoke
       except to give commands.

Most nights he was nowhere to be found –
       I would walk the empty rooms
crying for him, or go out into the road.

       Once a woman saw me on the bridge
and brought me home.
       After, he tied me to my bed with rope.

He lost all his money three times, burnt down
       our shop, the dogs trapped
below the galvanised roof.

       He gave me an orange, and we drove off.

He had a cousin across the river.
       A waterfall cascaded on the road
and my father carried me over.

He got married the first time in Mocho
       but I cannot recall the lady's name,
only she was nearly white.

Her father was McCormack. They had a baby
       and her name was Gloria.

He opened a new shop, bare shelves for months.
       We slept in the back with Linda Bloomfield.

I heard them in the night.
       I cannot recall if they were married.

He went to Kingston for days to play Mah Jong,
        came home angry,
beat me with his belt.

        I can still recall the heat and smell of him,
of sweetness and liquor.

        He had children in villages all over.
He got married to Bernella.
        I saw babies and never saw them again.

I held a baby called Zeta, my sister.

        Last time I saw him
he begged me for money.

        He was smaller.

The time before I'd held his gun
        to his head while he slept

but I didn't pull the trigger.

        He died in 1963 or 1964.
I can't remember.

Ran Away, My Mulatto Boy

(found)

Ran away, my mulatto boy GEORGE. Said George is six feet in height, a very light mulatto, brown curly hair, very intelligent, speaks handsomely, can read and write, will probably try to pass for a white man; is deeply scarred on his back and shoulders; is branded on his right with the letter H. Ran away the 27th February, a certain mulatto boy, 18 years old, **my heart is broken** named DAN. This certain boy **please dear god** appears nearly white, good strong teeth, **bring back to me** good countenance, fair curly hair, **my son** would nearly pass for a white person, has black eyes. Any person apprehending said boy and delivering him to me will receive a reward. Ran away, my mulatto boy FRED, an octoroon, fair complexion, though very sunburned, straight brown hair, grey eyes, a little crossed, about five feet four inches high, 22 years old. It is probable he has the marks of cupping or blisters on his breast and back, wears a size 7 shoe.

Topsy, Turvy

Turn me up and then turn me back
First I'm white and then I'm black

They in the museums now, in cool glass cases,
the dress rucked up, arms raised in horror-shock
by what's exposed: the black doll, head-scarf knotted
Mammy-style; the white doll with her gold wool hair
and sky-blue antebellum eyes. They lie
besides the stocks for runaways, chain cuffs,
an iron scold's bride. The frills of blouses hide
their needling, waist to waist and Siamesey
or like birth, head flopping from the other's body.

The sign relates the misery – of a mother
in the quarters' rush-light, stitching effigies
from scrap. To teach her little daughter *early* –
the way she'll learn the night from day, or come
to know her own reflection in the well –
how she'll be ripped away, to milk and coddle
in the old plantation house, and always have
two babies, one black, one white; how one must be
invisible when the other one's in sight.

Out of Many

That evening, I was Miss Mahogany,
between Miss Satinwood, Miss Ebony –
parading on the stage before the crowd,
my bust and waist and hip size read aloud,
skin polished as the venue's furniture –
old Bloomfield House, where May, my grandmother,
an octoroon, once scurried from her Master.
So close in looks, he must have been her brother!

Earlier we'd been gauged by tape measure
and shade chart, organised by skin colour.
Now that black was 'in' and beautiful
(no longer counting teeth or mapping skulls)
we darker girls in tropical bikinis
could join our paler friends. Miss Ebony,
in every photograph, bookends the row,
the darkest band of colour in our rainbow

shimmering on stage. A shame we three
of darker hues were named for sturdy trees
whereas our lighter sisters down the line
were fruit and blooms: half-way along, Miss Jasmine
and Miss Lotus Flower (Hakka grand-daughters
of Lowe and Chan, indentured labourers)
and smiling at the end, Miss Apple Blossom,
her golden hair arranged on pallid bosom.

The final round saw all the lovely Misses
sashay and twirl in satin ball dresses
and crowns of orchids – none of us exotic
as Miss All-Spice, her hennaed fingers beaked
like birds of paradise, a waft of perfume
as she danced. Then, in the bright-lit dressing room
we scraped the sticky make-up from our faces,
still in line, of course. We knew our places.

Borderliner

I'm skirting the bold lines of the map **border-liner, might mean white girl**
neither here nor there, but home in the border places **with corkscrew hair**
Tijuana, where rich American boys slam tequila **or brown girl with flat hair**
or controlled drugs, or down the fence **slipping from one side to the other**
where a veiled woman clutches her baby **always looking for the right light**
in the thin shadows **Passing, hoping the old world wouldn't catch her up**
always waiting to cross a *good day* or *hey girl* **in the wrong hotel or store**
I've always loved sea-swimming **some fool too loud, not seeing the signs**
but sometimes these waves carry **That kind of stuff could put you back in**
make-shift rafts bobbing empty of their cargo **chains or end with the blade**
below my feet, the sea-bed **but ever notice how green eyes in yellow skin**
cross-hatched with bones **look so good, how some faces have no borders**
There were times when these borders had **no fixed abode? You can sketch**
no barbed wire, and even now not all borders are **a pretty rainbow diagram**
so hard. There are places nobody cares to pass **or use faux scientific words**
Think of that frozen mountain trail where only a tin sign **to classify, or slang**
tells one snowy Nordic edge from another, or miles **relating to nation states**
of rough green march-lands **chocolate bars or animals – mongrel or mule**
where I have wandered for days **But I say it's only when you are standing**
That I'm home on the border doesn't mean **on the border that you are free**
I don't think about who took the world and carved it up **to look both ways**

54

Scott Joplin Rag

Black boys swinging from the pylons When my mother played *Bethena*
when you trod the dust from Texarkana on Sunday afternoons, I stood
No one wants a nigro pee-anna man down here boy! outside the door
Except the brothels of Sedalia Rag-time waltz for your dead wife, deep-
where your left hand turned into a fat toad belly bass-line, the top line
jumping steady on the bass notes yearning. I wanted to learn the piano
right hand twinkling for a quiet syphilitic girl just to play your music
always smiling in her peacock feather head dress It took me a decade
yellow skin and black eyes I wanted ruby-light saloons and poverty and
Missouri, piss-pit of never enough, your baby old-time ghetto glamour
dead at three months old Years later, I seduced a man in the piano room
Heard your screams downtown. Then Freddie of my American college
sweet Chrysanthemum girl, ten weeks wed playing *Breeze from Alabama*
who dies of a cold? You left her waltzing We danced, until our dancing
in the bedroom, one two three one two three was kissing, hands picking
puffed-up eyes, that red throat burning over each other like crabs. After
You took your ruined heart to the asylum we lay on the cool stone floor
A thousand toads bounced on the walls with nothing to say. I leant up
Some days your right hand grabbed your left above him on one elbow
the only way to keep it still smoking, like a scene from a Hollywood film

Note by Note

Asleep, Bird's fingers played my arm,
a new song, untangling.

Happy?
Something like it –

Kim and Pree and Baird,
the last two by him.

Corny stuff. Ice-cream and magic tricks,
sweet melodies he wrote them.

They photographed us
at our dinner table,

their cold meal a prop –
our 'integrated family'.

Always made do for myself:
the Cotton Club coat-check

or dancing on Swing Street.
Not my kind of man

but something I couldn't resist in him.
Then Pree's heart gone,

our small girl
and Bird killing himself

note by note.
I couldn't stay and watch.

Sincerely, Chan

Darling my daughter's death
surprised me more than it did you.

Don't fulfil funeral proceedings
until I get there. I shall be the first one

to walk into our chapel. Forgive me
for not being there while you were at

the hospital. Yours most sincerely,
your husband, Charlie Parker.

My darling. For God's sake,
hold onto yourself. Chas Parker.

Chan, help.
Charlie Parker.

My daughter is dead. I know it.
I will be there as quick

as I can. My name is Bird.
It is very nice out here. People have been

very nice to me out here.
I am coming in right away.

Take it easy. Let me be
the first one to approach you.

I am your husband.
Sincerely,

Charlie Parker

Mitchell/Mingus

'What's your favourite Joni Mitchell album?'

Everyone says *Blue*, but for me **My favourite jazz man? After Joe, I'd have to say**
it has to be *Don Juan's Reckless Daughter* **Charlie Mingus, as fat as the double bass**
two Jonis on the album cover, one in kimono and top hat **he played. Raised white**
one in drag, a blacked-up jazzster **until his mother said he was black and Chinese**
in a zoot suit and fedora. I stole it from a skate-boarding poet **Played cello the best**
in San Fran, my own reckless summer **but no room for black boys in the orchestra**
half drowned in the fat waves **Well if no one had his back, he'd back his own self**
of California or stewed on sours in the *Red Lagoon* **he'd shout his own damn name**
waking in whose room? I'd come home *Baron Mingus, Mingus Ah Um, Mingus!*
drink coffee, play *Off Night Backstreet* **Boasting of five wives, all those lovers, bad**
chords like car horns in the rain **temper conducting his fists, who knew America**
Didn't know music could be lyrical or dangerous like that **could hurt like this? When**
poor Jaco Pastorius staggering wildly down the bass **trouble came, his hands frozen**
'It's been stinger to stinger darling' **on the strings and one final album,** *Mingus,* **playing**
her voice in polyphonic layers **in his head, who'd he call? Joni, jazzster, she found**
sun-rays on the sheets of my small muddled bed **the words for him to say goodbye**

Genealogy

I carry you, a fleck, to Jamaica At the Chinese temple in Kingston
I am sick daily. At night Vincent leads me upstairs, says this floor
I hold the bed's rims was once full of beds where men off the boat
a raft on the rolling sea slept, ate, washed the sea-salt from their skin
You inside me, all this hope prayed at the jade altar with two lions
Sweet speck, what will you be? that too had shipped from China
Too soon to be anything We drive to the old cemetery, not before
I say nothing Vincent pays the wild-eyed boy who guards the truck
the way I stay silent He might hurt us, the vodka bottle he holds is
about my grandfather made from emerald glass. In 'New Superior'
who beat all his children I stand on my grandfather's wrecked grave
with a leather strap pen in hand. I am allowed to write his name on
The sun roasts the floor since it's been chiselled away, marble sold
I am woozy *Wow crazy day for you, huh?* Vincent smiles. A real honour
I don't know why I am here *to pay your filial duty to your Grandfather?*

High Yellow

Errol drives me to Treasure Beach **It's an old story** – the terrible storm
swerving the bleak country roads **the ship going down, half the sailors**
I think about what you will be, your mix **drowned, half swimming the**
White, black, Chinese and your father's **slate waves, spat hard on shore**
Scottish-Englishness. We cross the Black River **Smashed crates, bodies**
where they shipped cane sugar and molasses **choking on the dark sand**
upstream, past a sign **One man stands:** *What is this place?* A woman
for Lover's Leap. The air stinks of sulphur **in the trees, one hand raised**
Errol drops me at a green gate. *Be safe?* **This is how the Scotsmen came**
Behind the house, the narrow beach **why the black people have red hair**
of dark sand, the seawater warm and grey **Or the other story** – no storm
I am deep before I know it, groundless **no wrecked ship. Just the miles**
The swell stops the sickness **of cane fields and mulatto children named**
Under a crooked tree, perched on sea-rocks **McDonald or McArthur for**
two fishermen in torn denims, smoking **their fathers, who owned them**
I dry in sun. They pass, turn, come close **Nothing grows at Lover's Leap**
They've rust afros, gold faces splashed with freckles **where two runaways**
one edged in muscle, one with eyes **cornered by their master, held hands**
like razors. *What you want here* they say **and jumped down into the clouds**

Honey

There are no bananas in John Wong's **I've not seen my Uncle in twenty years**
and none in Kingston since **He meets me from the coach in his new red mini**
last year's hurricane flattened the plantations *Yes man* **he tells me** *I done well*
In the supermarket **Uncle Ken is 79 and still working. We drive to a cove bar**
the shelves are stacked with Hershey's and Nestlé **He drinks cans of Red Stripe**
Only the mangoes are home grown **with Mr Alexander. I lounge on a sun-bed**
I walk Dominica Avenue **watching the rocks that look like giant green turtles**
with pineapple yoghurt **and Ken, who has tan skin and snow-white hair, same**
soothing my stomach **father as my father, but Ken's mother was Amerindian**
which stirs and lurches with you inside. **They call him Honey but I don't know**
I am lonely **why. I remember his house, high up on the hill at Discovery Bay**
in Kingston **the fat mangoes I picked from the ground and sucked, puppies**
even the yellow walled hotel pool **panting under a tin roof in the midday heat**
reminds me how alone I am *I'm still there* **Ken says** *I build that damn house*
as I'm the only one who swims in it *you think I'll ever leave?* **We swerve back**
Uncle Ken said to go to **to the coach stop. Ken is drunk. Well that was March**
the back door of Lowe-Shu Supermarket, ask for Lee Chan **now it is December**
He'll tell me all about my grandfather but **an email says they found Ken's body**
Ken asks me *Good God, why you want to know?* **in his house, he had been murdered**

Brown Eyes Blue

Errol drives me to Red Hill. *Wild goose chase*, he says **Wally built the house himself**
but we find my Aunty Gloria behind rusted gates, lost **painted the walls lime green**
in a steep rock garden of tall clammy plants **He had thick yellow hair, oiled back**
She is child-sized, one spindly hand clamped on my arm **white shirt, bronzed skin**
blinking, *I know you? You know me? Wally dead, you hear?* **He liked old Country music**
Up in the house, the blinds ripped, books on the tiles **the back bedroom crammed**
a looking-glass leant on the door in two sharp parts **with his CDs.** *Wha' you think*
and Andrew, appearing from shadow in an *Irie* T-shirt *Jamaicans only like reggae?*
tray of mango slices in his hand, wet yellow smiles **He laughed.** *Don't tell me, you*
You came to live here with me, when? Gloria asks him *think all Jamaican folk are black?*
whispering to me *to cook and clean, but he does none of them things* **He was half Lebanese**
Later he shines the big black car **half French. After dinner he disappeared to play**
she can't drive anymore *Don't it Make My Brown Eyes Blue* **over and over while**
She pulls me to a garden wall **we sat outside with Gloria, my dad's long-lost sister**
where purple flowers grow, big and spongy **They laughed and drank rum together**
nothing I'd seen before. **The air cooled and a purple storm came over. I watched.**
I used to know all the flowers, she tells me. *I can't remember any more* **The more they talked**
whispering again, wide-eyed. *Can you save me?* **the more they looked like one another**

Yellow River, Milk River

(for Rory)

If you ask me about ancestors I'll tell you He weighted codfish down with salt **about Hakka people, always moving, hounded down** sold weevilled cornflour **from the mountains by knives** and turning milk, offered credit to the customers **and fire and blood** he robbed, his angry ticks and crosses in the yellowed ledger **to the Yellow River, to war** on the shop's back shelf. But the women in the salon **with the Punti** looked up when he passed by, believed his small bones made him *hakka*, **an insult spat until the Hakka took** tender, not a man to rope a child or **the word back; about tough land, bad water** stab a counter with a gutting knife **bad rice, moving on again: Guangdong, Fujian, Jiangxi** He had an inventory **of fortress villages, and the ships** of wives he withered in the country, fourteen **that carried the Hakka from the rim of** hungry children spread from Milk River **China to Surinam and Taiwan** to Yallahs Bay. The youngest boy, a bed-wetter **How *Hakka* became *guest worker*** he gave a dollar to and dumped, hitch-hiked **to Austria and Spain and Jamaica** to Kingston and survived. The only photo is **where my grandfather stepped off the boat** of his body, suited on a bed of silk **of Hakka men asleep in the bright lights** in the mahogany coffin he saved up **of the Chinese temple waiting for uncles and cousins** years for. One daughter **new lives. About my name, which is your name too** took it, for proof at last **from two ancestral villages, how there are eighty million Hakka people** that **scattered throughout the world, how I found this all out for you** he was dead.

Fifty Words of English

At night, we shared our words by oil-lamp.
Mother, sister, river, moon. Sleepless in our bunks
we swapped *sun* for *raincloud, work* for *home.*

On deck, we dropped our names into the sea,
took James or Sam, our careful tongues
performed the lines: *yes please Sir, good new life?*

Eleven O'Clock Child

I said *half caste* at school
before *half caste* was banned
and the next words came in

I was never half anything
just running the asphalt with my friends
bloody knees and hands

saving money in a jar
buried on the field
to fly away to America

didn't know about one drop rule
counting teeth, *hexadecaroon*
marrano, mestizo

Dad said his father called him
ship yit tiam
eleven o'clock child

I thought it was kind
not another way
to say unclean

Ship Yit Tiam

It's just a little heckle in the yard
Still love you, mule-child
mongrel of the shopkeeper and cook

My Chiney Royal
you're not quite noon
not midnight

stuck before
the clock's hands
reached the top

don't mean you
can't do maths
keep books

It's nothing
but a kink of hair
a lip poke

look of skin
cooked too long
not quite clean

What Charlie Said

Look, it's like this. You like dogs. You buy a dog. Let's say you buy an Alsatian. Huge ears, slobbering tongue, you know the deal. Let's say your neighbour's got a Chihuahua – poncey little dog, yap-yap, cross-eyed. Now they're both dogs, right? But they're different breeds. They're different species. You're not gonna mate them. No way you're gonna mate them. Cos what would you get? Precisely! It wouldn't be right, would it? I'm not a racist, but it's the same with humans. We're from different *species*, different *civilisations*. Some of us need to be out in the sun, so we've got black skin. Others live where it's cold, like this poncing country, so we're white. Then you've got your Indians, your Pakistanis, job done. I don't mind 'em coming here, but we're not meant to mate, no way. I've read a book about it. I've *thought* about it. It's not about race, it's the same with dogs – we're just different breeds. Like your dog, Chloe, she's sweet but she's not pedigree. Not the best she could be, is she? Exactly! I've known your dad half my life but oh we've had some rows about this one. I told him 'Chan, look it's like dogs – no reason not to get on, just don't mate them!' But he sits there in his armchair, lights his cig and looks at me – like I'm a fool, like *I'm* a bleeding idiot!

What Do I Remember of Sofia?

She came one Christmas day in a snow tiara
and we sunk into the sofa in a snarl of leggings
and leg warmers and laughter. In my room,
I showed her all my *care bear* stickers, played
Cyndi Lauper on the tape recorder, while she picked
at the edge of my wallpaper and gently ripped
each lemon rose, until the adults found us
and she blamed me

        and in the frozen garden
she wore my earmuffs, and pretended to skate
on the icy footpath, and I thought shouldn't *I* look
like you, Sofia? Erica her mother
was white like mine, her father Jean was black
like mine and Sofia was the beautiful colour
of toffees I banged around my mouth till it bruised
and her hair was a golden poodle of curls

        and we promised
to write each other letters, and I did write
and sent Sofia a tube of glitter, but never
had a letter back, and soon stopped thinking of her
in Geneva (where she lived in a wooden house
on the whitest hill among the alpine trees
and on blinding days of sun and sleet and snow
glided calmly out onto the frozen lake –)

If You Believe: In the Smoke and the Light

If you believe I met my father in 1964
at the hideaway on Eden Grove,
his hand on my arm as I walked through the door,
young man in a black shirt and tailored suit
and I knew his face of course
but we'd not met before, you may as well
believe anything I dream of,
searching through old photographs –
the way he looked up close say, still like a boy
with his bright skin and loose laugh,
tapping his foot to the band's brash sound
as we sat at the bar with the poets and crooks.
You may as well believe we danced a number
to a softer tune, a girl at the microphone,
her voice wrapped tight around the horn
and after, slipped out across the street
through the gates to a Victorian square,
so strange to be walking with my father
in the cool autumn air, his coat on my shoulders,
hand at my back, and just talking talking
of his life before – of mongoose and snake,
the Yallahs River, his father's store,
his father's belt, the ship that sailed him here.
There was an old clock, a cracked fountain,
and as we walked I saw people like us
on the benches, shapes in the dark,
heads bent close and talking talking
and back in that hot cellar dive, I danced all night
with the Ghanaians and Trinidadians
and a French man who spun me with great virtuosity
and I was as fast and wild as the child I'd been
at the community hall in my ballet shoes
dancing dancing, *pas de chat, girls, your feet are wings!*
And my father was sat in the smoke and the light,
a woman at his side with coaled eyes,
her red lips split wide with laughter
and I think she was my mother –

Old Daisy-face

Old Daisy thinks the day breaks in the night,
wakes singing and waits for the blinds to lift
and the show to begin. I guess night-time's a gift
of riches: police lights in the street, a fox fight,
the flickering stars. Old Daisy-Face sings louder,
his hot little hands in the air – thinks he's stopping
the moon from falling down, a pale ball bopping
from hands to head, that big moon keepy-upper.
Me and his daddy slog the long night through.
We sing, we pace, we rock and roll mad Daisy,
we try to feed him quiet. But that old crazy
just shuts his petals when he's ready to –
then it's show over, done, whole face sealed tight
and turned away to shun the morning light.

Notes on the poems

WHAT IS PLAY IS OUT THE WINDOW!

The late Joe Harriott was my father's first cousin, and also my mother's boyfriend for a time.

The title of this section, and the last line of 'Sax II' are based on the following comment by Harriott: 'I don't want to equal. I want to be superior. All the others... they play inside the room, in here. What I play is out de window, out de window!' found in Hilary Moore's *Inside British Jazz: Crossing Borders of Race, Nation and Class* (Ashgate, 2007).

Alan Robertson's biography of Harriott, *Fire in His Soul: The Joe Harriott Story* (Northway, 2011), was invaluable to the writing of these poems.

Song for Shake (17) is loosely based on Philip Nanton's article 'Real Keane' in Caribbean Beat, 2004.

Partita, 1968 (19): 'Partita' is the first track on the 1968 album *Indo Jazz Fusions I* by Joe Harriott and John Mayer. *Raga* (Sanskrit): meaning literally 'colour, hue' but also 'beauty, melody'.

What Is and Isn't Jazz? (20) Adapted from 'Abstraction or Distraction' by Daniel Halperin, a review in in *Jazz News*, 1961.

Mingus (24): Charles Mingus broke off his UK tour to travel to Southampton to visit Harriott in hospital. They had never met but Mingus arrived late in the night and was refused entry. Harriott died shortly afterwards.

Alpha Boy (25): Joe Harriott was left at the Alpha Boy's Orphanage in Kingston, Jamaica when he was ten years old.

If You Believe One Pale Eye (28): Chan Canasta was the stage name of Chan Mifilew, a well-known television magician in the 1950s and 1960s. My father was nicknamed 'Chan' after Canasta, because of their shared dexterity with playing cards.

ORMONDE

Many of these poems draw on the small archive (newspaper coverage, photographs and the passenger list) about the voyage of the SS *Ormonde*, which sailed from Jamaica to Liverpool in 1947, a year before the better known *Empire Windrush*.

Passieras (34): The term 'passieras' is borrowed from Sam King's testimony in Mike and Trevor Phillips' *Windrush: The Irresistible Rise of Multi-Racial Britain* (Harper Collins, 1998): 'We were Yard People, we didn't use the word Yardie, we used the word Passieras, we were going to club together and we were going to survive.'

Boxer (35), **Dressmaker** (36), **Schoolboy** (37) and **Stowaway** (40) have their genesis in the Ormonde passenger list, where passengers were required to list their occupations.

Distressed British Seamen (39): The term 'Distressed British Seaman' refers to any seaman who finds themselves without a ship in a foreign port.

Mishra's Blues (44): The title is taken from the 1969 album *Indo Jazz Suite* by Joe Harriott and John Mayer. The story of Misir and Luther is adapted from a story in my father's notebook about his childhood friends.

BORDERLINER

'Borderliner' is a derogatory term for someone of a mixed-race background.

My Father's Notebook (39): Adapted from text of a notebook written by my father about his early life in Jamaica.

Ran Away, My Mulatto Boy (51): The non-bold text is taken from notices placed in newspapers seeking the return of runway slaves in Jamaica in the 19th century.

Out of Many (53): In 1955 the 'Out of Many, One' beauty contest was held in Jamaica. Its theme was 'Glorify the Jamaican Girl – Ten Types, One People', and featured ten winning girls from different racial backgrounds, classified by the shade of their skin.

Note by Note (56): The right-hand side text is composed of the four telegrams Charlie Parker sent his wife, Chan, on learning on the death of their daughter.

Fifty Words of English (63): Chinese immigrants arriving to Jamaica at the beginning of the 20th Century were required to pass a written test to demonstrate that they could write fifty words in three different languages.

Eleven O'Clock Child (64): 'Ship Yit Tiam' is a slang term for mixed Chinese and black Jamaican children, probably no longer in use.

MIX
Paper from
responsible sources
FSC® C007785